# ADVANCED DEER HUNTING

## JOSEPH MILLER

authorHOUSE®

*AuthorHouse™*
*1663 Liberty Drive*
*Bloomington, IN 47403*
*www.authorhouse.com*
*Phone: 1 (800) 839-8640*

*Published by AuthorHouse 10/17/2019*

*ISBN: 978-1-7283-2996-3 (sc)*
*ISBN: 978-1-7283-2995-6 (e)*

*Print information available on the last page.*

*Any people depicted in stock imagery provided by Getty Images are models, and such images are being used for illustrative purposes only. Certain stock imagery © Getty Images.*

*This book is printed on acid-free paper.*

*Because of the dynamic nature of the Internet, any web addresses or links contained in this book may have changed since publication and may no longer be valid. The views expressed in this work are solely those of the author and do not necessarily reflect the views of the publisher, and the publisher hereby disclaims any responsibility for them.*

This book is dedicated to the Good Lord, my Savior Jesus Christ, and the Holy Spirit who blessed me with a loving family, great friends, and the opportunity to hunt trophy bucks.

# Contents

# Introduction

Experienced hunters know there is nothing more rewarding than harvesting a trophy buck. Hunting is a challenge, it is not an easy sport. Deer hunting is very unforgiving, and any small mistake can cost you a big buck. The keys for successful hunting are preparation, attention to detail and understanding deer. This is not a how-to-book for deer hunting that teaches you how to shoot with a gun or bow or a book that repeats common sense rules. Rather, this book shows why we, experienced hunters do things in a certain way to successfully harvest that trophy buck.

# Chapter 1
# Preparing to Hunt

As experienced hunters, we know that the better prepared we are for deer season, the more successful we will be. Therefore, let us review the things we need to do prior to hunting and the reasons for doing them.

## Finding the Best Area to Hunt

A critical part of deer hunting is choosing the right place to hunt. Just going out to any wooded area does not work to harvest a trophy buck. Big bucks like to live in woods where there is a healthy balance of wildlife. A healthy balance of wildlife means there are a variety of trees and plants, different types of food sources, and plenty of wildlife. Wildlife often includes squirrels, raccoons, coyotes, bobcats, hogs, owls, turkeys and of course, deer. Having a nearby water source is also a definite plus. As you start to recon an area for hunting, look for signs of a healthy balance of wildlife.

Most experienced hunters have a prime location to hunt.

But if you lost your deer lease or moved to a new location for a better job, then you need to find another place to hunt. There are basically four types of hunting areas from which to choose: your own land, someone else's land (deer lease), public land, and high fence game ranches. Each has different rules and regulations that must be learned and followed.

The best place to hunt is on your own property. On your own land you can practice firing your bow or rifle, hang your own feeders, plant your food plots, and place your deer blinds wherever you choose. You control who hunts or does not hunt on your land. And the best thing about owning your own land is that you can pass it down to your children and grandchildren. The downside to owning your own land is that you have to maintain and pay for it.

Paying to hunt on someone else's property is what we refer to as a deer lease. This is the most common land to hunt for most hunters. You can find deer leases advertised on the Internet, in the local newspaper, or by word of mouth. When selecting a deer lease, take into consideration the rules, price, location, overnight facilities and the production of large bucks. The location or distance from your home to the deer lease can be an important consideration. If you like to hunt after work during the week you may not want to drive long distances to your deer lease. A deer lease may have a high ratio of hunters to hunting acres which leads to higher hunting pressure on the deer. This might result in the deer moving more at night than they usually do. It is also important to check out the hunting rules of the deer lease. Some deer leases permit you to shoot any deer while others have strict control on the size of the bucks you can shoot. Most deer leases will permit you to hunt with corn and deer blocks if legal to do so. Deer leases may also have food plots, feeders and deer blinds already established. In addition, check out the deer lease's rules for behavior. You don't want to be a member of a deer lease where you feel uncomfortable taking your son or daughter if there is excessive drinking, bad language, drugs, etc. Deer leases are by invitation only. So while the members are checking you out, check them out as well. Deer leases are great for bonding and you can make some friends for life by becoming a member.

Public lands such as national forests are great places to hunt and have some pretty big bucks. Hunting permits usually do not cost much and the forests are patrolled by Game Wardens. Before you start to hunt on public land ask a Game Warden where the best areas to hunt are located. Game Wardens are usually helpful to friendly hunters who obey the rules. Speaking of Game Wardens, remember to wear blaze orange and don't have a loaded rifle in your truck as this not permitted on public lands. Also, most public lands prohibit using any kind of baiting such as corn or deer blocks. The biggest problem encountered while hunting on public lands is that you never know when another hunter will walk in your hunting area. This problem is very frustrating as it can ruin your morning or afternoon hunt.

The last place to hunt is a high fence game ranch. Hunting in a high fence game ranch offers hunters an excellent opportunity to harvest a trophy buck. You can find their ads on the internet or in the local newspaper prior to hunting season. A guide will usually accompany you to a predetermined deer blind and assist you in selecting which buck you can harvest. The major down side of hunting on a game ranch is the price. Harvesting a 12-point buck costs more that harvesting an 8-point buck. Make sure you have the price in writing before you shoot a large antler buck.

## Choosing the Right Clothing and Equipment

Having the right clothing and equipment is very important before you begin to hunt. Clothing depends on the weather in your area. That is, hunters in Wisconsin or Michigan need to dress warmer than hunters in Florida or South Texas. You need to have at least three sets of hunting clothes for deer hunting.

The first set of clothing is for scouting. Scouting for deer signs involves walking in the woods prior to deer season. When the weather is warmer you will need to wear clothes, gloves, cap and boots that are light weight and breathable. Make sure your boots have rubber soles so that they leave as little scent as possible on the ground. Also wear light gloves to avoid leaving your scent on vegetation in the area. Always wear a hunter's orange cap or orange vest when you are scouting. Deer cannot see orange but trigger-happy hunters can. I also recommend wearing an orange cap with a mesh backing while walking in the woods in warmer climates. Much of your body heat escapes through your head; therefore, the mesh cap will help keep you cool when the heat escapes it. Remember to spray a scent killer on all your clothing, gloves, boots and hat prior to walking in the woods. Finally, it is best to scout just before it rains, as the rain will wash away any scent you might leave.

The second set of hunting clothes is for bow season. Bow season usually occurs during the Pre-Rut period when the weather is warmer. As such, this set of clothing needs to be light and breathe well. Keeping your clothes scent free for bow season is crucial as you will be shooting deer that are 30 yards or less from your deer stand or ground blind. Wash your clothes, gloves, and cap in scent free detergent and hang them outside before and during bow season. By hanging your clothes outside, they will absorb the smell of the woods and not the odors inside your home or garage. Since the deer will walk very close to your stand you must be well camouflaged for bow season. Wear a greener pattern of camouflage that matches the leaves in the trees in the early fall.

The third set of hunting clothes is for rifle season. Rifle season is normally during and after the Rut and Post-Rut periods when the weather is much colder. Therefore, dress in warm comfortable clothes in layers and that breathe well. Wear a browner pattern of camouflage that matches the leaves in the trees in the late fall and early winter. Experienced hunters know that keeping your feet and hands warm are the biggest challenges in cold weather. For my feet, I wear soft rubber boots with thick socks and arch supports. For my hands, I wear leather gloves with wool or cotton inserts. Another item I put very high on my cold weather list is a soft, thick camouflaged hood that keeps my head warm and serves as great camouflage. Just remember to wash it in unscented soap before, during and after the hunting season.

Choosing the right equipment for your hunting trip

goes hand in hand with being prepared. There are many miscellaneous items you should take with you when you go hunting. Be careful not spend a fortune when you buy these items.

Each year I buy a small, inexpensive camouflaged backpack as my old backpack might have a stale odor from last year's deer scents. Equipment you should put in your backpack include: a sharp hunting knife with an orange lanyard so you can easily spot it if you drop your knife in the woods; a small powerful flashlight, a compass and your muted smart phone. It is good to carry your smart phone with you to the woods in case of an emergency. However, don't rely on your smart phone as the battery could die, there could be no signal, you could lose it, or it can get wet. The flashlight and compass app on your phone should only serve as a backup to your hand held flashlight and compass. Also include in your backpack two bottles of drinking water, a laser range finder, a deer/grunt call, deer scents in an air tightly sealed bag, a small roll of orange or pink deer tape to help you mark a blood trail, lighter or matches in case you need to make a fire and most importantly, a pen with your hunting license in a zip lock bag, and most importantly, toilet paper. Experienced hunters know that toilet paper is very important as you never know when you have to dig a hole and use the bathroom in the woods. Many of us who fought in Iraq understand this problem. In addition, bring an empty bottle with a wide top to pee in. Some hunters claim it does no harm to pee from a deer stand. I disagree. I believe if I can tell the difference between human urine and doe or buck urine, then a big, wise buck can smell human urine and will steer clear of my area.

## Understanding Deer and the Rut

Experienced hunters know deer have excellent defense mechanisms against predators in terms of smell, sight and sound.

Smell or scent control is the biggest concern for bow hunters. If a buck can detect your scent, he will stay away from your location and you will never know that he avoided your area. There are many common sense articles and internet videos that emphasize the importance of being scent free and using the wind to our advantage. That is, hunt from a stand where the wind is blowing into your face. None of us can never be 100% scent free and sometimes there is no wind. To mitigate my human scent, I wear scent free camouflaged clothing and apply scent killing spray on my hunting clothes. I also apply a small amount of cover scent around me that matches the buck or doe scent I put in front of my stand. After doing these things, I have does and bucks walking under my stand.

Not being visually detected by a deer is tough to do when bow hunting. Deer have excellent 320 degrees vision and can detect any movement even when you are in a 14-foot ladder stand or climber. You must minimize any movement when bow hunting. When a buck comes within shooting range of your stand, you must slowly move your compound or crossbow to your firing position. In addition, deer are not color blind. They can see one half of the color spectrum. This means they can see short and middle wavelength colors such as blue and green, but can't see yellow, orange and red. Therefore, I don't recommend wearing blue jeans in a deer stand.

Deer have big ears that are directional and are always listening for any sound of a predator. Make sure you do not make any man-made sounds when you are climbing or sitting in your stand. Also, frequently drink small amounts of water to avoid coughing or clearing your throat.

Much is written on how lunar phases and weather effect deer hunting. Experienced hunters time their feeders to go off early in the morning and late in the afternoon. These times generally coincides with deer lunar activity. My observation over the years is that during a new moon deer move more in the early morning and late afternoon. During a full moon, deer move more in the late morning to early afternoon hours. Deer move less during the first quarter of the moon. Additionally, there is more deer movement in the afternoon during the last quarter of the moon. I also check my cellphone app for the major and minor peaks in lunar activity. I see more does in the first half of a lunar peak followed by more bucks in the latter period. For example, if there is major lunar activity from 0700-0900, I will see more does from 0700-0800 and more bucks from 0800-0900.

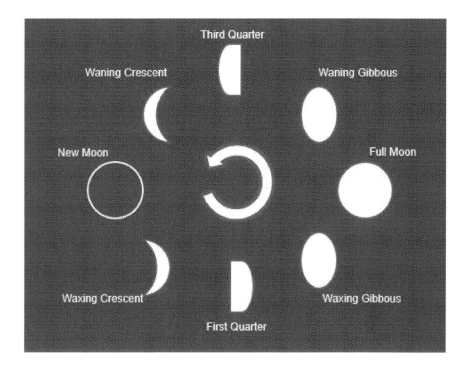

In regards to weather, the general rule that deer move more when the temperature gets colder stands true. That being said, I have harvested a few really nice bucks in warm weather. In addition, I see more deer activity just prior to and after a hard rain. Furthermore, it's always good to be in a deer blind during a light rain.

It is important to understand the Rut before you hunt. Experience hunters know deer go into a rutting or mating season in the fall. This is called the Rut. The best way I found to understand and how to hunt the Rut is by dividing it into three periods: Pre-Rut, Rut, and Post-Rut.

Pre-Rut is three weeks period prior to the Rut and coincides with bow season. The summer heat is finally abating, and the mornings are getting cooler. The leaves are still on the trees and are starting to turn colors. The acorns are starting to turn brown and are beginning to drop. During Pre-Rut the bucks begin to walk around in the woods during daylight hours in order to recon and mark their territory. Bucks mark their territory by rubbing their antlers on small trees. The longer the rub usually means the bigger the buck. Bucks also are prone to fight each other during this period.

Rut is usually in the peak of autumn when the leaves and acorns are falling from the trees. Rut is when does come into heat and are ready to mate. This drives the bucks crazy. To quote my fellow combat veteran and great hunter Jeff Townsend, "It's a magical time of the year!" Rut normally coincides with rifle season. Experienced hunters will stay in their deer blind as long as possible because bucks throw caution to the wind and chase does anytime during the daylight hours.

Rut occurs as the daylight begins to shorten in the fall. This is called the photoperiod. The shrinking ratio of daylight to darkness causes a chemical change in does that increases their melatonin production and brings them into heat or estrus. Bucks make scrapes and chase does who are in estrus and are ready to breed. They will chase, breed and stay with a specific doe for a 72 hours period before moving to the next doe. This mating period which is referred to as the Rut can last up to four weeks as not all does come into estrus at the same time. Experienced hunters know there will be a seven to ten day peak period of the Rut when many of the does go into estrus. This is the time to take off from work and be in your deer blind.

During the Rut period, I've found using doe in estrus scents and loud doe bleats work best. I have also observed that there is an intense Rut every three years. For example, in 2017 we had an intense Rut as big bucks ran carelessly after does during daylight hours. Even though Rut is initiated by the shortening of daylight or photoperiod, I believe that an intense Rut coincides when a full moon is closer to the first of November.

Post- Rut is the month after the rut when deer are hungry. Bucks are more likely to be seen in the early morning and evening hours. The few does that did not breed during the Rut will go into estrus for a three-day period 28 days after the peak of Rut. This three day period during the Post-Rut is a good time to use doe in estrus scents. I have found that doe scents and grunt calls are not that effective during the remaining weeks of the Post-Rut period. I have been more successful being quiet and scent free in the Post-Rut period. I also change my tactics and hunt over hot deer trails that lead between the feeding and bedding areas.

## Scouting for Buck Signs

One of the most enjoyable aspects of deer hunting is scouting for buck signs in the woods. Finding buck signs is exciting. Plus, scouting is good exercise to walk up and down hills and breathe fresh air. I recommend bringing a fellow hunter or a friend with you to scout the woods. Going into the woods with another person is always safer in case of an accident. Plus, scouting with a friend will pump each other up as you share the excitement of finding buck signs. If you do not have anyone to scout with you, always inform someone where you will be. In addition, you can also ask a Game Warden where to hunt. As I mentioned earlier, most Game Wardens are helpful to hunters who follow the rules.

Once you have arrived at a section of woods where you want to scout, park your vehicle in an easy to find location and lock it. When scouting in the woods always wear hunter orange. Some states require so many inches of solid hunter orange when scouting or hunting, so check the rules prior to going to the woods.

It is very easy to get lost when scouting, so bring a map,

compass, smart phone, reflective tacks, and orange tape. Remember to periodically mark where you have been so you don't get lost as it can happen to the best of us. Tear off a 12 inch piece of tape and tie it on an overhead branch every 100 yards. You will retrieve your tape after you are finished scouting. If you do become disoriented in the woods, turn around and retrace your steps back to your vehicle.

When you begin scouting in the woods, look for acorns, deer trails, rubs and scrapes. As soon as you find a rub or scrape, tie a piece of orange tape over it to serve as a temporary, easy to see reference point. Scout the immediate area for a hundred yards in every direction for other rubs and scrapes. This will enable you to determine where the rub line or scrape line is located. Make sure you retrieve your orange tape as you do not want to leave it there for other hunters to see your buck signs.

As I scout the woods prior to deer season, I focus on finding a rub line. A rub line offers the best chance to see bucks during the Pre-Rut period and in the first week of Rut. After the first week into the Rut, I change my scouting tactics to search for scrapes. Even though bucks usually visit their scrapes at night, experienced hunters know they might get a big buck when the buck checks his scrapes early in the morning and late in the afternoon. After the Rut, I change my tactics and scout for an active deer trail in the Post-Rut period. An active deer trail is well travelled and will have fresh deer tracks and droppings on it. These trails usually connect the bedding areas to the feeding areas.

Once you found a rub line, scrapes or a deer trail you will hunt over, check your compass. Determine the direction of the prevailing winds and look for a good downwind location from where you will hunt. Determining the direction of the wind is critical as every successful hunter knows to use the wind to his or her advantage. Keep in mind that warm air rises in the morning and cool air descends in the evening. This will impact the spread of your scent; therefore, hunt from a higher location in the morning and a lower location in the evening.

If you are hunting during bow season, pick a good tree that is 20-30 yards from the deer trail or rub line. This is the maximum range you should use for bow hunting. When you are hunting during rifle season, pick a good downwind location as far away from the deer signs as possible to place your deer stand, portable climber or ground blind. Be careful not to disturb or touch the area near the rub or scrape. Bucks will notice anything out of place and will avoid the area if they detect your scent. For that reason, it's best to scout your hunting area just prior to a rain. Also, never leave your portable climber overnight in your hunting location. Leaving your portable climber may spook away the deer who are walking the woods at night. Plus, other hunters might take your stand if they find it.

Now that you found a place to hunt, find another good location. That is, always have a secondary place to hunt. You never know when someone might beat you to your hunting area if you are hunting on public lands. Plus, hunting in the same location for too many days will leave your scent in the area.

After you select your hunting location, retrieve the orange tape that you used to mark the rub line or scrape. Retrieving the tape will ensure you won't advertise the location to other hunters. Next push reflective thumb tacks into both sides of a few trees leading from your stand and back to your vehicle. This will enable you to use your flashlight to illuminate a path to and from your stand in the hours of darkness. Place the tacks two feet high on the trees leading from your truck to your stand and four feet high on the other side of the trees returning from your stand to your truck or All-Terrain Vehicle (ATV). Furthermore, you need to use reflective tacks to mark the location of your parking place. The woods look very different at 5:00 am in the dark than during daylight hours.

Game cameras are extremely useful for scouting. Game cameras show us the date, time, temperature and a picture of the does and bucks when they travel on a deer trail or visit a scrape or rub line. This type of scouting can provide us a pattern over time that we can take advantage. Two types of game cameras primarily exist on the market: cameras that require you to retrieve the photos from them and cameras that automatically send the photos in real time to your smart phone. Of course the former are less expensive than the latter. Both types of cameras require rechargeable batteries and both need to take pictures with infrared light and no flash. I recommend placing your camera approximately five feet high on a tree about 20 yards from the deer trail, scrape or rub. If you place your camera near your feeder, be prepared to receive a lot of photos of squirrels, raccoons and hogs.

**Food Plots and Feeders**

Planting food plots, green fields, and activate feeders is beneficial prior to the hunting season. Food plots or green fields are excellent food sources that can attract deer for the entire hunting season. The best location to till and plant a food plot is next to thick woods that are a safe distance and direction from any roads or houses. Power lines that cut through the woods are ideal locations for food plots. Remember to get permission from the local power company before planting a food plot under them. Weather permitting, the best time to plant or plow your food plot is four to six weeks prior to deer season. Before planting your food plot, take a sample of the soil to your local county Agriculture Extension Service to have the soil tested. The Agriculture Extension Service can determine the best fertilizer for you to use. I also recommend planting a good blend of seeds that will attract deer. Rye grass, clover, winter wheat, winter peas, oats, and beets are just some of the plants you can include in your food plot.

I use two types of corn feeders to attract deer: a tripod feeder and a hanging feeder.

A tripod feeder can hold and dispense a lot of corn which is good to bring in more deer. I place my tripod feeder in an open field near thick vegetation where there are no trees and as far away from my deer blind as possible. If you place your tripod feeder in the middle of an open field, you will most likely only attract only does and hogs. In addition, placing your tripod feeder in the woods under tall trees will make the feeder vulnerable to raccoons and squirrels.

For my hanging feeders, I hang them near a major deer trail. I also put the feeders downhill from my deer blinds and as far away as possible. I set the timer for the corn to spray for three seconds when the morning light is bright enough for shooting and one hour before it gets dark in the evenings. For example, at our ranch in South Texas, the feeders will go off at 7am which is first light and at 5pm which is an hour before dark. Make sure the lids on the hanging feeders are secure as raccoons will do their best to tear them off at night to get to the corn.

# Chapter 2
## Bow Season

Bow hunting is the most challenging method of hunting a trophy buck. It is also, in my opinion the most rewarding. Unlike hunting a buck with a rifle, you must hunt a buck with a bow at close range. Bow hunting will require you to control your scent, movement, and sounds which is hard to do when a big buck is walking 20-30 yards away from your stand.

**Compound Bows and Crossbows**

Our son Jordan, of whom my wife Debbie and I are very proud, loves to hunt with a compound bow. I am older with a few Army injuries and therefore, prefer to hunt with a crossbow. Every hunter has his or her own preference. Whether you prefer a compound bow or a crossbow, choose the one that you can easily draw back the string, has good speed for the arrow or bolt (at least 370fps), and shoots quietly. The bottom line with bows is to use the bow that you are comfortable with and practice, practice, and practice before bow season.

When I practice with my bow, I apply a fresh coat of lubrication to my bow string and confirm my zero. Using a laser range finder, I shoot a thick square bow target to confirm my zero at 20 and 30 yards. Next I shoot my decoy deer at 20 and 30 yards from my 14-foot ladder stand. My son uses a compound bow and does the same procedure at 30 and 40 yards.

I do not recommend shooting a deer at more than 30 yards for two reasons: Even though you will likely hit the deer with your arrow at a distance greater than 30 yards, the arrow will take longer to kill the deer. This might result in the deer walking around with an arrow stuck in it. Secondly, it is more challenging to track a deer that has been shot with an arrow at a distance greater than 30 yards. Sometimes the blood trail does not begin until 50 to 100 yards after you hit the deer. So, if you shoot a deer 30 yards or less with an arrow, then you have a better chance of finding the blood trail and recovering your deer. Plus, when I shoot a deer with an arrow I want it die quickly without suffering for a long time.

Where should you aim to kill a buck with an arrow or a bolt? When I shoot a buck with a rifle, I aim for the heart or the neck for a quick kill shot. For a bow, I've found that bucks are easier to track with a lung shot. A lung shot results in more blood and bleeds quicker than a heart shot and consequently, makes it easier to find the blood trail and locate your buck.

## Stands, Climbers and Ground Blinds

There are primarily three ways to hunt deer with a bow: using a ladder stand; a portable climber; or a ground blind. Each has its advantages and disadvantages. Even though experienced hunters have their own preference, I think it is important to review these options as you might say "I never thought of that". This might lead you to try a different method from which to bow hunt that will increase your success.

Ladder stands are the most popular means to bow hunt. Ladder stands can be either portable or stationary. Ladder stands should be at least 12 feet above the ground and require you to wear camouflage that blends in with the leaves around you.

The advantage of the portable ladder stand is that you can set it up at different locations. This method gives you more options for hunting locations and keeps the deer off balance as to knowing your location. The disadvantages of a portable ladder stand are that you have to carry it in the woods and set it up in the dark for a morning hunt. Also, a portable stand is less stable and comfortable than a stationary ladder stand.

The advantages of the stationary ladder stand are that it is tightly secured to a tree, you don't have to carry it around in the woods, and it is comfortable. The main disadvantage of a stationary ladder stand is that the deer know it is there and may avoid the area. Therefore, it is important to position your stationary ladder stand in a concealed location from a major deer trail. It is also a good idea to have two or three ladder stands from which to hunt. That way, you don't leave your scent in one area. If you order a ladder stand online, I recommend you order the two-man stand. The two-man ladder stand has enough space for one hunter to tie down a backpack and bow next to him without feeling cramped for space.

Portable climbers give bow hunters the advantage of hunting bucks from different locations. I love to hunt from my portable climber. They are easy to carry on your back and they don't have any steps of a ladder that the deer can see. When using a portable climbing stand, always wear your safety strap or harness. The disadvantages of a portable climbing stand are the noise the stand makes when you attach it to a tree and when you shimmy up the tree. In addition, you have to find a straight tree that is not too wide or narrow 20-30 yards from a deer trail or a rub line.

The third method of bow hunting is from a ground blind. A ground blind should be placed in the shadow of a tree and camouflaged with bushes and branches. The less conspicuous a ground blind the better. Place your ground blind in a good location from a major deer trail at least three weeks prior to the Pre-Rut. The advantages of a ground blind are that you can sit in a comfortable chair without any danger of falling to the ground, move around a little bit, and not be seen by a deer. Plus, a ground blind is a must when you are bow hunting in a light to medium rain. Experienced hunters know that bucks move during a light and medium rain. The disadvantages of a ground blind are the limited fields of vision for the hunter, scent control, and movement control. You are eye level with the deer which means there is an increased chance they can see and smell you if you make any sudden movements. In addition, you can get a little claustrophobic when sitting in a ground blind.

There are other ways to bow hunt that I did not discuss. They involve hunting in the open either walking or stationary. Hunting in the open increases the chance deer will either see, smell or hear you. If you choose to hunt in the open, I recommend you use a crossbow and sit on the ground with your back to a tree 20 yards from a deer trail. Have your crossbow ready to make a quick shot.

**Effectively using Deer Calls and Scents**

Many hunters use deer calls and scents to successfully lure bucks to the hunter's location. We see this on hunting shows quite a bit. I prefer not to use any deer calls or scents but rather to remain invisible in terms of smell, sound or sight. However, if I do choose to use deer calls and scents, I do so sparingly. Moreover, my tactics differ between bow and gun seasons.

During bow season bucks are in the Pre-Rut mode and are marking their territory for the Rut. Bucks are not attracted to the does yet, so a doe scent makes no sense to use. However, bucks do not want to share their territory with other bucks, so putting out buck urine will make a buck investigate if another buck is in his territory. When I use a buck urine scent, I place it about three feet off the ground and 20 yards in front of my hunting position.

Bow season is also a good time to rattle in a buck. Bucks are prone to fight each other over territory, so a little light rattling works well. I like to use a couple of old deer antlers when I rattle as these make the authentic sound of deer fighting. If I don't have any old antlers available, I will use a rattling bag or artificial deer antlers that I purchased from an outdoor sports store. About 30 minutes after there is enough daylight to shoot, I will rattle lightly for 20 seconds. I will pause two minutes and make a couple of soft, short grunts spaced ten seconds apart. Now I wait ten minutes to see if a buck comes to me. If I don't see a buck, I will lightly rattle again for another 20 seconds. I then wait an hour and repeat the grunting and rattling. I do not rattle or grunt anymore after that. When I see a buck, I softly grunt again and see if he moves toward me. I only grunt when he is standing still and never while he is moving towards me. Sometimes when I grunt, I will make a deep soft sound of a buck grunting through my mouth instead of using my artificial grunt call. I know this sounds a little crazy but it actually works.

If I hunt the next day, I will change my rattling and grunting pattern and start an hour instead of 30 minutes after first light. Deer are smart so it is important to keep them off balance. A wise buck can tell the difference between a hunter and another deer.

## Shooting a Buck

When I walk to my stand either during bow or rifle season, I use a flashlight. Once I walked to my stand without a flashlight and I found out this was not a very smart thing to do. I came upon a very large wild hog who grunted at me in the pitch dark. Hogs are very dangerous plus I didn't have a gun but only my bow on my back. All I could do was grunt as loudly as I could to make the hog run away. A couple of weeks later, I made sure to use a flashlight when I walked to my deer stand and came upon a skunk about 20 yards in front of me. I shined my flashlight in its eyes to make the skunk run off. I can only imagine what would've happened if I had walked right up to that skunk in the dark.

When I am about 30 yards from my stand, I slow down my walking and take a few steps and stop. I wait a few seconds, and then take another few steps. This makes me sound more like an animal in the woods and not a human predator. When I get to my bow stand, I tie my bow and my backpack to two separate 20 feet ropes or 550 cords that I have hanging down from the top of my stand. (A 550 cord is an olive drab thin rope that you can purchase from your local Army-Navy store. I highly recommend it.) I put out my buck urine 20 feet from my stand on two pieces of brown napkins three feet off the ground. I then slowly climb up the stand and am careful not to make as little noise as possible. Once I am sitting in my stand, I silently grab the rope or 550 cord and slowly pull my bow and backpack to me. I make sure I secure them to the top of my stand with two separate three feet pieces of rope or 550 cord. Now I am ready to hunt.

When a big buck walks within range of my bow stand, I take my time shooting the buck for three reasons:

- The first reason is to verify the exact range from me to the buck. For example, if I think a buck is 30 yards from me, but in fact, he is only 25 yards away, then my shot will be too high. Or if I think the buck is 25 yards from me but in actuality is 30 yards, then my shot will be too low. To mitigate the risk of over or under shooting my arrow, I use a laser range finder to determine the distance of surrounding landmarks such as a deer trail, bushes, trees, etc. that are around my stand before I see a buck. So later, when a buck walks in front of my stand, I will already know the exact distance from me to him.

- The second reason I take my time before shooting a buck is that the buck can easily pick up any movement I make when he is close to my stand. Therefore, I have to move my bow very slowly to my firing position when the buck is looking in another direction before I take my shot.

- The third reason I take my time to before shooting a buck with my bow is to ensure my point of aim is exactly where I want my crosshairs to be. As I stated earlier, I prefer to place the arrow in the lungs so that the buck will bleed more readily than if I shot him in the heart. Therefore, I take my time to aim for lungs which are about eight inches below the back of the neck. This shot location also makes it more difficult for the buck to either duck under or jump over the arrow.

## Tracking and Recovering your Buck

When I shoot a buck with an arrow, the buck will normally bolt to one side and run off. I will then wait in the stand for twenty minutes before I get down. This delay helps the buck think no one is following him and consequently, the buck will stop running and sit down to die. If I follow him too soon, the buck will keep running for a much greater distance since he knows a predator is pursuing him.

Once I climb down from my deer stand, I will do a thorough search for the arrow on the ground. If the buck jumped or ducked out of the path of the arrow, then I missed him and I'll find the arrow in the ground. If I hit the buck, I will mark the location where he was standing by hanging a one-foot piece of pink/orange tape from an overhead branch. I'll then walk in the direction of where the buck ran and look for the first drops of blood. It may take me up to fifty yards before I find the first sign of blood. I will mark this spot with another piece of tape and continue to look for more blood until I find the buck. Bucks and does normally run in a downhill direction toward thick vegetation after being shot. Do not be surprised if the blood trail leads you that way.

Experienced bow hunters know that tracking a buck after you shot it with an arrow can be very challenging. Once I find the buck on the ground, I will drag him under some shade and tie another piece of tape above him. Then I will get my ATV and retrieve him. If I am by myself, I will tie the antlers of the buck to the back rack of my ATV and drag him back to the deer camp for field dressing.

# Chapter 3
# Rifle Season

Hunting a buck during rifle season is very different than hunting a buck during bow season. Unlike bow season which is during Pre-Rut, rifle season occurs during Rut and the Post-Rut periods. Therefore, your hunting tactics have to change in order for you to successfully harvest a trophy buck.

**Deer Blinds, Stands, and Hunting on the Ground**

The majority of gun hunters hunt bucks from deer blinds and deer stands. A deer blind is an enclosed wooden or metal box stand that has windows for hunters to detect and shoot deer. Blinds are best placed on a hill that overlooks a funnel or tree line at a distance of 100-200 yards from the deer blind. It is good to have more than one deer blind from which to hunt. This will ensure you can use the wind direction to your advantage. Unlike a bow stand, deer blinds minimize the chance of deer seeing and smelling you. Some deer blinds have two chairs which are ideal if you want to take your son or daughter hunting with you. There are three very good reasons why experienced hunters prefer to hunt bucks from a deer blind during rifle season.

- First, deer blinds provide concealment, comfort, and to some degree warmth during the cold weeks of late fall and early winter. Deer blinds need to be located as far away as possible from where you expect the deer to move and eat. This will minimize the likelihood deer will see, smell, or hear you. Sometimes it is necessary to clear some branches in order to see deer at a long distance from your deer blind. Bucks like to move in areas of thick brush and trees. Plus, they will notice if their natural habitat has been disturbed. So only trim branches and vegetation that are higher than six feet off the ground. This will give you a clear shot from your deer blind at a long distance while at the same time keep the thick vegetation and the bucks in your area.

- The second reason hunting from a deer blind is ideal during rifle season is that during the Rut, bucks can be seen chasing does anytime during the day. You therefore, need to be in your deer blind for as long as possible. This means you need to be comfortable and be able to move around to some degree.

- The third and most common reason deer blinds are popular is that they provide protection against the weather. Experienced hunters know deer move when it's cold and wet. When you hunt for long hours in a cold and wet day, you want to stay as warm and dry as possible.

An ideal location to put your deer blind is on a hill overlooking your food plot. Deer will normally visit your food plot at night and in the early morning or late evening hours of daylight. Does will venture out in the middle of the food plot while the bucks will remain near the trees on the sides of the food plot. So when you see does entering your food plot, scan the edges of the food plot for big bucks.

Deer stands are open wooden or metal stands that allow hunters to sit in a comfortable chair 12 feet or higher above the ground. I prefer deer stands to deer blinds as I feel like I am sitting in a tall throne overlooking the deer below. Plus, I can enjoy looking at all the nature that surrounds me. Deer stands are best placed on high ground in thick woods where a close-range shot is your only option. However, deer stands are not conducive to cold and wet weather. Also, you must be careful to minimize your scent and movements while hunting in a deer stand.

Hunting from the ground is an effective way to harvest big bucks. You can either hunt from a stationary position or by walking around. Remember to always wear hunter orange when hunting on the ground. The major advantage of hunting on the ground versus deer blinds or deer stands is that the deer do not know where you will be located when you hunt on the ground. They do however know where the blinds and stands are located and will try their best to avoid them. The major disadvantage of hunting on the ground is that you are eye level with the deer and thus, they can readily see you. Also, your field of vision is significantly restricted compared to hunting from an elevated deer blind or deer stand.

Use the terrain and weather to your advantage when you hunt on the ground from a stationary position. For example, deer like to cross powerlines. Locate the major deer trail where the deer cross and select a place on the high ground where you can sit next to the tree line and overlook the deer trail. Make sure your location is as far away and downwind from the trail as possible but also from where you can make a good shot. Then walk across the powerline and select another spot by the tree line. You now have an early morning hunting location and a late afternoon hunting location where you will be concealed in the shadows of the rising and setting sun. Place a log at a 45 degree angle in front of you so that you can rest your rifle on it when you take aim. Another example of finding a good location to hunt on the ground is to locate a hot deer trail and sit on the ground with your back to a tree 20-30 yards perpendicular from the deer trail. Have your rifle or shotgun in your lap and be ready to quickly shoot a big buck when he walks past you.

Walking in the woods with a rifle or shotgun is an effective and enjoyable method to hunt bucks on the ground. If you choose to hunt with a rifle when walking in the woods, I recommend that you use a peep sight rather than a scope. A peep sight enables you to quickly aim and hit a moving buck. The best way to hunt deer when walking in the woods is to hunt with a 12 gage shotgun. A shotgun will give you a quick aim and shot. I use either a 3" or 3 ½" 00 buckshot. I also recommend you hunt with a dog if it legal to do so in your state and county. One of the best times to walk in the woods is after you and your son or daughter have been sitting in a deer blind for a few hours. They will enjoy the feeling of stalking the woods and scaring up a late morning big buck out of a thicket.

It is good to have more than one deer blind and deer stand to hunt from during the Rut. Use the wind to your advantage. For example, if the wind is blowing from the west, hunt in the deer blind that is located in the eastern part of your lease. Also, if your game camera picked up a trophy buck in a certain area, hunt for that trophy buck in a nearby deer blind or stand in the seven day peak of the Rut.

## Hunting during the Post-Rut

Deer hunting in rifle season also means hunting in the Post-Rut period. The primary mating season is now over and the does and bucks are hungry. Post-Rut is when the weather is very cold and all the leaves have fallen from the trees. Experienced hunters know that hunting in this very cold weather is a challenge. The best locations to hunt are overlooking chokepoints or funnels where the terrain channels deer movement. The best times to hunt these areas are early in the morning and late in the afternoon. This is when the deer are moving to and from their feeding area to their bedding area. If your deer blind and deer stand do not overlook a chokepoint, then I recommend you select a good ground location over a hot deer trail. A hot deer trail has fresh deer tracks and deer droppings on it. If you chose to hunt on the ground, bring a warm soft pad to sit on and carry a wool blanket to wrap around your body. A blanket will trap your body heat around you.

During the Post-Rut period, does and bucks are likely to visit your feeders in the early morning and late afternoon. This is a good time to hunt close to your feeders. If your deer blinds or deer stands do not overlook your feeders, then create your own food source to attract deer. There are a lot of concoctions on YouTube that people enthusiastically proclaim attract deer but in reality don't work. What I found to be highly effective and inexpensive to make is what I named Buck Mix. Buck Mix is a large plastic jar of peanuts and apples mixed with a small amount of peanut butter and inexpensive pancake syrup. Empty half of the peanuts from the jar into a bag and then add cut up apple pieces to the remaining peanuts in the jar. Stir in one teaspoon of peanut butter and syrup. This will add a strong, sweet smell to your peanuts and apples and will attract deer faster. Cut two small holes in one corner of the jar and tie it to a tree with a four foot rope or 550 cord. This will prevent deer and hogs from moving it away from your area. You can also hang your Buck Mix in a tree about four feet off the ground so that it doesn't attract hogs and ants on the ground.

## Effectively using Deer Calls and Scents

Using deer calls and scents in rifle season is different than using calls and scents in bow season. In bow season, the bucks are in the Pre-Rut phase and are walking around in the woods marking their territory. In rifle season, bucks are in Rut and are chasing does to mate. Therefore, you must adjust your calls and scents to meet the buck's needs. As I stated in the previous chapter, I normally hunt without any calls or scents in order to be invisible to the deer in terms of smell, sound and sight. However, when I choose to use deer calls and scents I do the following:

I place two small pieces of a brown napkin three feet high

on a branch near a deer trail or a rub line as far away from my blind as possible wearing plastic gloves, so I don't leave any scent. I then apply a liberal amount of a doe in estrus scent on each piece of napkin and return to my blind. I put the plastic gloves in a zip lock bag and then put on my hunting gloves. I wait for an hour to see if any deer come into the area. I will use my deer call to blow a couple of loud three seconds doe bleats about ten seconds apart and repeat this each hour. I will also add a couple of short soft grunts an hour after the sunrise and 30 minutes before sunset. Once I am finished hunting, I retrieve the brown napkins and throw them away. This ensures I will always use a fresh napkin for each hunt.

In Post-Rut I do not use any scents as the bucks and does are focused on eating. The only exception for using scents is during the three day period the few remaining does that did not get bred during the Rut go into estrus. This three day period is 28 days after the peak of the Rut. If I chose to use a deer call, I will grunt softly a couple of times during the morning and evening hunts just to send a message that the area is safe for deer.

**Hunting with a Rifle**

Choosing the right rifle is a personal preference. I recommend a 243-caliber rifle for women and teenagers as this is a high-powered deer rifle that doesn't have a big kick. As for myself, I will hunt bucks with a 30-06, a 270, 30-30 or 7 mag. The rifle I choose is based on which blind or stand I will hunt, the weather and the terrain. I like to hunt with my 30-06 rifle with a 3x9x40 scope that fires a 150 grain Remington or Federal bullet. This is my all-purpose go to rifle as it has good range, good accuracy and good knock down power. If I am hunting in an area where the bucks usually move at a fast pace, I use my AR 15 with a soft hunting round. The AR 15 has a peep sight which is ideal for shooting moving targets. Also, it's always good to have at least one rifle with a synthetic stock to carry to your stand when you are hunting in a light rain.

Always confirm the zero of your rifle before deer season. Just because your rifle shot accurately last season doesn't mean it will shoot accurately this season. Scopes can get bumped. When I zero my rifles on our ranch, I put a paper target on a tree 25 yards from a steady firing position. Once I adjust my shot groups to hit the bullseye, I place three full, two-liter plastic coke and sprite bottles adjacent to each other 100 yards away and shoot the middle bottle. The bottle explodes at the impact of my bullet. This reinforces my confidence that I will hit the buck in the right place when rifle season arrives. Shooting a moving buck requires a different skill than shooting a stationary buck. I practice shooting moving targets by shooting predators such as coyotes, wild hogs, and bobcats with my AR-15 prior to and after deer season.

**Shooting and Tracking your Buck**

When you enter your deer blind or deer stand do so very slowly. Pay attention not to bump your rifle against the walls or floor. Once you are in the blind, do everything in slow motion and focus on being silent. Bucks will notice any unfamiliar sounds and will stay clear of your area.

When you see a trophy buck in rifle season, shoot him as quickly as possible. Do this because bucks tend to move faster during the Rut compared to the Pre-Rut. If you wait for a better shot, your buck may be out of range or in a thicket before you know it. In rifle season, aim for the heart or the base of the neck so that your shot drops the buck in place and you don't have to track him. Just be careful to slowly raise your rifle to your shoulder when the buck is not looking at you and take a steady, smooth shot.

Wait in your blind for at least ten minutes before you get down to track and recover him. This will give the buck time to run and then lie down to die. Mark the spot where you shot the buck with a piece of orange tape tied to a branch. You can see this spot by the deer prints that are dug into the ground when the buck bolted to one side. Follow the direction where the buck ran and mark the first sign of blood. Then go to the next sign of blood and mark that as well. Now you have a clear direction to follow and find your buck. Remember that deer usually run downhill after being shot with a bullet or an arrow. Once you located your buck, drag him to some shade and mark the spot with two pieces of orange or pink deer tape on an overhanging branch. Get your ATV and a fellow hunter to help you retrieve your buck. Take a photo of your trophy buck and securely load him on your ATV. Return the buck to your Deer Camp to field dress him. And finally, take him to the meat processor and the taxidermist.

## Field Dressing, Processing and Mounting your Buck

If your state requires you to tag your deer, then fill out the tag and attach it to your buck's antlers as soon as you have shot it. That is why you include a pen with your hunting license in your backpack. Do not let a Game Warden walk up and find that you haven't tagged your deer yet. The Game Warden might get the wrong impression.

I recommend taking your buck back to your Deer Camp to field dress him. There you can hang the buck to neatly field dress him. If you choose to field dress him in the woods, then you might get blood all over you and your ATV. Plus, you will probably get small pebbles and dirt in your deer meat. I can personally verify that is not good thing. I bit into a piece of goat meat in Afghanistan in 2009 and lost half my tooth to a small pebble.

You can cut up the deer yourself or take it to a deer processor. I have done both as one method is messy and free while the other method is convenient but costs money. Before you take your buck to a processor, do some homework to determine which processors are reputable. Most deer processors are trustworthy and will give you back the meat from the deer you killed. The processor will also cut your deer into the pieces of meat you desire. This includes the back strap, tenderloin, hamburger, cube steak, sausage, and left-over trimmings to make deer jerky.

If you shoot a buck with a big set of antlers, you will probably want to have it mounted on your wall. Make sure you tell the deer processor that you want to have your buck mounted. I recommend you tell the processor you want a shoulder mount. This will ensure the processor leaves plenty of the deer's cape for the taxidermist. Take your deer to a reputable taxidermist who can show you the different types of mounts that are available. Look at the quality of his work, price, and waiting period for him to complete the mount. Some hunters shoot a buck with a rack so large that it can be registered with Boone and Crockett. The rack will be issued a score and will be entered into the official records. Many hunters have the antlers mounted on a wooden plaque. Most hunters prefer a neck or shoulder mount that is with or without a plaque. I prefer a shoulder mount with a plaque and the deer looking to the right or left at a slight angle. Before you select the type of mount, consider where you think your trophy buck will look good in your home or office. Also take in consideration where your spouse will let you put your mount in your home.

## Cooking and Enjoying your Deer Meat

There are many books and YouTube videos on how to prepare and cook your deer meat or venison. Deer meat is tender and tasty when properly cooked. Some people like a deer's natural gamey flavor when eating their venison. I don't care for this taste. Therefore, I take the following steps to remove the gamey taste when I want to cook deer steaks: I take the meat out of the freezer and let the meat thaw out. Then I beat the venison until it is tender and cut it up into the small steaks. I soak or marinate the steaks in a marinating steak sauce for a couple of hours which removes the gamey taste. I put foil on an open grill and lay out strips of bacon. I then add sliced pieces of onion and bell peppers and place the deer meat on top. The deer meat will absorb the flavors of the bacon, onions and peppers but will not touch the hot skillet or foil. I will turn the meat over after a few minutes and ensure the inside is done but moist and tender. I'll empty all the contents into a shallow bowl and serve with rice pilaf. My family and friends really enjoy this meal.

You can also cook your deer meat on the grill as shish kabobs. Stick a metal shish kabob rod into the meat, small tomatoes, onions, mushrooms, and bell peppers and coat them with olive oil and garlic powder. Place the kabobs on the grill and be careful not to overcook the meat. Add rice pilaf and enjoy your shish kabobs.

Frying cube steak or thin cuts of the back strap is also delicious. After you have beaten your venison, soak it in milk in the refrigerator for a couple of hours. Drain the meat and add some fresh milk. This will remove the gamey taste. Dip each piece of meat in flour sprinkled with pepper and garlic salt. Lay the meat in a skillet with hot cooking oil and fry the steaks until each side is golden brown. Avoid overcooking and serve with green beans, mash potatoes and gravy. You and your family will enjoy a very tasty meal.

Deer jerky is easy to make. There are many tasty ways

to make jerky. One of the simpler methods is to cut up the meat into thin strips and season with black pepper and a little bit of the red peppers that you sprinkle on a pizza. Lay the strips on the racks of a dehydrator and cook for about eight hours. Remove the meat and let it dry in the open to remove any moisture. Drop your jerky in small bags and share with family and friends.

# Conclusion

I hope you enjoyed this book and learned a few things that will help you enjoy a safe and successful hunt. Remember, deer hunting is a challenge, but the reward is great when you harvest that special trophy buck. God Bless and Good Hunting!

Printed in the United States
By Bookmasters